A Collection of Poetic Polaroids on Life, Love and Loss

For a Life without Loss is oft one without Love.

Deepa Patel

BookLeaf Publishing

Presentation by *BookLeaf Publishing*

Web: www.bookleafpub.com

E-mail: info@bookleafpub.com

ISBN: 9789357444989

First edition 2021

DEDICATION

For the ones in my life that I love, have loved and lost along the way.

A life without loss is oft one without love.

ACKNOWLEDGEMENTS

Would like to thank the people whom without I would have given up on myself. Life's an individual journey but I wouldn't have made it this far without support, laughter and most of all- love.

My family and friends are everything to me and also I wouldn't have started writing poetry or drawing or creating birthday cards were it not for the love I have for them. Which led me to the publishing of this book.

Refusing to mention all the names (you know who you are!) and are beautiful to me inside and out…without a doubt. So thank you.

...And to whoever spends their hard earned time to purchase this and maybe even peruse a page or two!

1.The Beginning/First of Poetic Endeavours. The One about My Love.

It started off as many things do- almost innocently,
A small conversation at work about football leading inadvertently,
To late night Facebook chat and banter,
Even a football commentary chat canter,
Resulting in compliments of her being 'quality',
And admiration of his greatest trait of honesty,
Talk came of Sunday dates,
As 'more than mates',
Into a 'date rules',
Game or few of pool,
Ensuing in devouring his roast dinners,
Which was a sure fire winner!
Alas! Though things seemed near perfect,
And though she knew he was worth it,
There was a short delay,
For making it official before she went away,
But he realised upon her departure,
That she was the one he was after,
And so bright and early on 2015 New Years Day,
Unlike any previous January 1sts you could say,
He made a 5am trip to pick her up from Heathrow,
Not realising from this trip what could grow,
Finding love and relationship unfold,
Love greater than these words could told,

Like a scene from 'heart actually',
A gesture worthy of the pull of gravity,
She felt; as she walked towards him,
Smiling to the brim,
He felt it there was an opportunity,
She felt a strong sense of unity,
And sealed the deal with a kiss,
Cause never did she ever feel like this,
Three weeks later he would proudly utter,
Three little words she could only at first mutter,
Words still true, simply declaring 'I love you',
And am in awe of everything you do,
Even less than a few weeks after,
She was granted a meeting with his daughter,
An official offer so cute,
With a matching sweetheart to boot!
Twas familiar phrasing,
'My baby's so amazing',
And 'I love you lots of loads'
Through all the crossroads,
Even when my tongue is in knots,
It's easy to reply, 'And loads of lots',
Not so easy is to explain,
Just how he drove her insane,
So sweet, so true, so much fun,
A feeling of this couldn't be undone,
Weeks of love and laughter,
And a couple of months after,
They moved into his familial home,
A safe place for love to roam,
Together they went for meals,
Usually pertaining steak deals,

And ventured forth to mini breaks away,
In Sunny Brighton for short stay,
A couple who's competitive streak,
Her winning was no easy feat,
She lost at pool, golf, darts and bowling,
And though he was always consoling,
She (finally!) succeeded,
In Mario Kart and was even undefeated,
A record that still stands,
Confirmation by a shake of hands,
Through the good times and bad,
He always made her happy when previously sad,
In him she found the greatest boyfriend,
And his broken heart she would mend,
And her insecurities he would rebuild,
And at last they were both fulfilled,
Loved and supported,
Never feeling unwanted,
She was grateful for the way she feels,
Making her heart and tummy do cartwheels,
So...this is a long and rhyming way,
For me to say,
I love you loads each day,
and to wish you a very happy anniversary!

2.The One about Tears/Emotions.

You got tracks,
Following the facts,
Born in heart,
Emote apart,
Coursing like veins,
Drabs like rains,
Ebbing endlessly,
Shunting detrimentally,
Like a heart and tears,
Beyond beats and years,
Always and forever.

3.The One about Trauma and those that Inflict it

Sometimes I wish I wasn't me,
So damaged and so small,
Neuropathways unwired,
Divided in what feels like constant road works,
Highway of pain,
Tear ducts overworked,
Knee jerk rejection shirked,
Easy to be overwhelmed,
Uneasily helmed,
Heightened sense of emotion,
Anxieties inflated,
Amgalyda swelled,
After effects of trauma is not so easy,
But then again neither is love.

But then again, I'd rather-
Be literally any other,
And just be me,
Instead of you,
Any day of the week,
I get no twisted sense of pleasure,
No sadistic kick,
In fact it makes me feel quite sick,

The idea of fight(ing) out a pique,
The idea to purposefully make someone else feel weak.

4.The One about Anxiety

Time and it all just moves slow,
When you all you can do is frozen in fear,
While all else surrounds seems to flourish and grow,
No matter how frantically you grasp to hold dear,
You're paralysed by time,
Fear of the future equally looms,
As the pasts lessons give no reason nor rhyme,
Everything engulfs and consumes,
Eating away at each thought,
Gnawing at core and spirit,
No safety from the storm- there's just no port,
No sense of consolation, conclusion or merit,
All that remains is overwhelmingly immobilised,
Also known as anxiety in disguise.

5.The One as Eulogy for Nani (Grandma)

The world had an amazing 83 years with you,
83 years of love,
In what you gave and would do,
For one and for all of us,
We were blessed for you to be our **Nani**,
The fond godmother and **Foi** to all,
We all have cherished moments to recall,
Of you bossin it in kitchen,
We always said as mother hen,
You could have earnt a mill,
As a head chef with talent and looks to kill,
Most significantly though as our amazing **matriarch**,
Also fond memories involving an Aussie shark,
But will hark on that in a mo...

83 years as a tribute and testimony,
And today's beautiful ceremony,
And these mere words,
Will never feel enough.

You led a life loved, loving and well-travelled,
And we loved that you travelled well,
Also through struggles and strife,
We know you still had an amazing life.

You also gave us grandkids our gifts of creativity,
In many different ways,
See our creative abilities in seas,
Or oceans of genius or (at very least!) waves,

For **Reena** dances true to form,
And **Radhika** bakes up a storm,
Anand's kindness in his genuine ideas,
Vishal creates so much love,
As the baby boy of the grandkids after so long,
We showered him in the love,
He kindly gifts back,
And embodies a bit of all the above,
Including bake offs with **Radhi**,
He's also arty like me,
All the best of us all from **Nani** we can see,
Many of the things we so proudly be.

Sometimes a traditionalist,
Sometimes a radicalist,
You would be a trad wife,
And suggest I make **Patchy** dinner instead of
surprise you on your birthday,
A day and moment I will treasure,
Beyond any measure,
But then also walk a dangerous walk,[1]
Less safe and stand up to the talk,
Be radical and still work,

---

[1] There's a legend war story of when my **Nani** walked through **London** through a bomb scare.

As a machinist and seamstress,
You made and designed our (and our Dolly's) matching dress!

We will also always remember so much,
Precious moments and such,
The moment of fear and joy,
When you heard of **Reena's** first Xmas premature boy,
And the photo of you green screened with a shark,
Your face so expressive,
Your love too, is so impressive,
It touches our **heart** and leaves a mark,
That memory cannot fade,
It's such a shame,
To say goodbye and your name,
But we will never feel ok,
So instead we say- see you again,
Our **Nani, Ba, Mum,Bhen, Mami, Kaki, Foi,** and **Friend,**
Until our souls meet you and **Nanna** again.

6. The One as a Eulogy for Del. R.I.P

You are Forever...
A SON...
A BROTHER...
A HUSBAND/SOUL MATE...
A FATHER...
An UNCLE...
A FRIEND...
And will always be A LEGEND.

You are only gone from our eyes,
Never gone from our heart,
I know you hear our cries,
Can't understand why you had to part,
From the biggest part in our lives,
You brought such joy,
Always knew when he arrives,
The One and Only **Del Boy**,
With his special knock,
And presence so full of energy,
It is still such a shock,
But we will remember thee,
Our hearts and memories cannot forget,
Your love, life and laughters,
And all you leave us yet...

Precious features in your **daughters**,
Not forgetting your beautiful **wife**,

And soulmate of 21 years,
Whom you dedicated your entire life,
Shared all your experiences and fears,
Our fear came true the day you left,
Taken too soon,
Was nothing short of a vast theft,
Causing a path of destruction like a typhoon,
Or even the storm the weekend after,
That god awful day,
Thunder reverberating like disaster,
On the 22nd May,
You broke your siblings's hearts too,
Such a loved brother,
And forever a **Chelsea** Blue,
They'll never be another,
They even retired your cue...

You were more than just a great friend,
First, you were a beloved first-born son,
Even though **Jackie's** love for you will never end,
Your brotherly love too, can never be undone,
For **Stephen, Kerry, Patric**k and **Jade**,
Such a strength of love,
That will never ever fade,
You were also an amazing **Uncle** to a lucky brood,
To **Charlene, James, Scott, Jake, Joshua, Jordan, Stevie, Alex, Emily** and **Maisy**,
Blessed were they to have an **Uncle** that was such a dude,
That constantly made them laugh like crazy,

Your pride and joy are your girls and role as the most devoted doting dad,
To **Faith**, **Elle** and **Brooke**,
No stronger **Father** they could have ever had,
And we can never forget the love you took,
And that you placed so tenderly,
In your wife and soulmate,
A love that will safely remain,
Alive, well and will radiate,
In your beautiful **Charmaine**.

No safety from the hurt,
In the storm, you left no port,
And though we will cling to each other for support,
We will always miss you **Derek Gary Watson-Short.**

7.The One about Memories

I don't wanna forget all the 'in-jokes',
I don't wanna forget all the moments and laughs,
Or forget each caress and strokes,
The moments preceding the photographs,
Each tender embrace,
The way my heart felt,
Bursting in a race,
Blessed feelings dealt,
I wanna capture each moment,
Hold it all still,
In perfect bestowment,
Recall the intensity of will,
To be in this perfect moment with you,
Relive it all and on repeat, as I say I do.

8.The One about being 'Alonely'

Sometimes I just want to be alone,
Finally, a logical emotion I can condone,
Isolate myself with all the pain,
Where there is no truth or feign,
Space to just be,
Unequivocally- just be me,
Just thoughts to think,
Thirsts just to drink,
Heart just to feel and to beat,
Emotions to just feel is no easy feat,
A place to just deal and to be-at,

Hole up between doors of despair,
Where I can I just have space to not care,
Say I just don't give a shit,
That's definitely just it,
But the moment I get it,
All that seems to hit,
That being alone is all that's there,

Deafening silence also,
Nowhere to hide or go,
Brimming at the seams,
Not even a space for daydreams,
The only thing that is stuck,
And source of my headfuck,

Is all that's there in my head and heart.

Maybe this is why and what it means,
That it is true, all is never as it seems,
And we never really are alone,
A thought to hold close and to own,
That also might bring some comfort,
As someone will always be with you even
when you feel most alone.

9.The One for a Friend Who's Been in Hell and High Water

I wish for you to feel the love you have for others in yourself,
I wish for you to see yourself through my eyes,
I wish for you to have all the wonderful things in life,
That ironically you deserve above all else because of your pain and strife.

It was never right or just,
It was always unfair,
But take from this you must,
You deserve the best care.

From the world to shelter the storm,
My wish for you is a haven,
Safety in a port,
Until my wishes come true,
I will stand next to you,
As your friend and 'till the end,
And always as a support.

10.The One as Ode to a Little-known Sporting Team!

Sounds crazy but it's true,
But football saved me,
Always a Red even when feeling blue,
Not only the feast of eyes to see,
But also, to feel,
The chants are in my heart,
Not only a skill but an art,
Tis all so real,
At either home or away,
The beat to feel,
Put simply- it gave me a love I would say,
A passion for the beaut game,
No other team for me,
Even a blind woman could see,
The spark of devilled fire within my eyes,
Alight and aglow,
Seeped in poignancy yet strikingly in snow,

For every season
And every reason...
And Always,
United Forever.

11.The One About Vows

Love me with quiet ferociousness,
Hold me like it's the last time,
Squeeze me like it's the first,
Care for me like family,
Have patience like a friend,
Loyal like a pup,
Honest as a child,
Be thoughtful with your words,
And be meaningful with actions,
Make me laugh,
Wipe my tears,
Be there through trials and tribulations,
Share my joys and accomplishments,
Revel in my victories as if they were your own.

And I promise I will for you too, my love.

12. The One with A **Gogo's** Love

-Dedicated to a wonderful friend Patronella (Gogo) on her birthday.

Shona's affectionate name for **Grandma** is **Gogo**,
And what a wonderful Gogo her babies have!
With so much love to feel and show,
It cannot be described as a share or half,
For **Gogo's** love knows no measure,
As for always and for forever,
Her **Grandbabies** are her greatest treasure,
And her love is unable to deter,
Measured beyond compare,
The strength of bond,
And she is equally aware,
Like the love for her child can only correspond,
Her love runs deep,
Like a river it just flows,
Like a mountain it is steep,
A bond that constantly grows,
With each and every passing day,
Her immensity of love,
Is always present-a fixed point to stay,

Peaceful as a dove,
Fierce and strong like a lion,
In the face of everything is her love,
Felt in her every atom and every ion,
And the love Gogo has for **Malachay** and **Myah**,
Knows no limits and no bound,
Emblazoned with passion like fire,
As cliché as it may sound,
There is nothing Gogo would not do,
To keep them both safe, sound and loved,
And prevent them feeling blue,
Away from hurt or any harm,
Her protection can never be undone,
Enamoured by their innocent wit and charm,
Gogo's outpour of affection knows no beginning or end,
Same as the unconditional love from their Uncle Roy's,
Actions from education about United and football,
To spoiling them with clothes and toys,
To running to their every call,
And anything to hear their laughter,
And fill the home with a warmth of contentment,
Document precious time by photograph,
Proudly on display for presentment,
At birth they bought the family together,

Strengthened by such small bundles of joy,
Continued memories to remember forever,
To cherish, soak up and enjoy!

Words for **Malachay** and **Myah**,
To **Gogo** you are both perfect,
No greater ambition to aspire,
You make every sacrifice worth it,
Your mere mention results in,
Gogo's face to alight and glow,
As her most precious kin,
And her eyes warm and a-gloat,
Filled to the brim with bliss,
For you both- her love and soul's sweetest kiss!

13.The One about Specters

They say there cannot be an absence-
Without a presence,
You've haunted my life,
Like a spirit drifts in,
And a ship setting sail,
'Passing' through,
You were there divided,
Like ‘Schrödinger's Cat’,
Half-blessing, half-curse.

Burn and crash, then repeat,
Expecting an uncanny return,
But to an extend you did,
And still remain to,
Just not as I envisioned,
Not a presence,
Nor an absence,
Just there.

There in a passing thought,
Fleeting,
Juxtaposed as equally a constant,
Like a metronome,
Beating,
Like heart and mind,
Entangled and intertwined,

Components of Soul,
But I'm done fighting the storm,
No longer a soul-dier,
Like the ship that set sail,
Possibly fated to fail,
I lend my heart,
And white flag,
Captured and defeated,
I surrender and set you free.

14. The Untitled One

Pencil taxing instead of taxiing,
Fear of flying,
Fear of falling,
Fear of failing,
What is it all though?
Ornithophobia was the songbird,
Away to a place away from home flight,
Fright of Flight,
Though on second thoughts maybe it was derived by envy,
Simply put but of the ability to leave,
Away and faraway from or toward Home,
Maybe it wasn't as first thought, and wasn't ornithophobia all together?

But oneirophobia,
Daydream of freedoms,
Keeper of Edens,
Reality of prisms of prisons,
Catnapping through life,
Lies wide shut,
Fear of driving,
Driving me mad,
Nomad woman no longer in attic nor box room,
But angry in defiance,
Furious and I love it,

Owning the feeling,
So oft denied,
Fury- I love,
Fury- I own.

Tying to Eire my charm,
Not for a Boxer,
Nor a second,
Not taste for ear,
Tying to a Ty-Son,
And also enticing my senses from slumber,
I no longer shudder,
My pencil can't work any harder,
Than my cluttered thoughts,
Overworked,
Previously weapons of mass distraction,

Now alive in their unwell and unrest,
Still in fear but atleast no inaction.

15.The One for Radhika and Tom (who met at Specsavers)on their Long-awaited Wedding Day

Love is Blind...

Or so they say,
But on your wedding day,
I think it may be short-sighted,
To think you might be so blighted,
Or at very least slightly blurred,
To not see what has occurred,
The joining of two people,
Meeting at a symbolic steeple,
Or rather a registry,
A 'mandap' expressively!

Also it would be worse than astigmatism not to see,
How beautiful it is to agree,
And how blessed you both are,
To have family and friends near and far,
To witness your lovely vows,
And hearing of wows,
As **Radhika** walks down the aisle,

A lifetime of waiting for **Tom** would be worthwhile,
To finally see her on their special day,
A moment sure to take his breath away,
From the 7 steps and vows of marriage,
A symbolic horse and carriage,
Exchange of your banded rings,
As the Geet song sings,
It is a Tale as 'young' as Time,
And to not notice would be a crime,
That **Radhi** will always be a **Belle**,
And who in love did she befell,
No other than **Tom**- though not a **Beast**,
Though can animalistically still devour a feast,
And also a black belt in Taekwondo,
Still a Prince Charming though,
For on their 4th year,
He took a leap of faith in fear,
To await the answer,
To a question to advancer,
And share rest of his life with his honorary princess,
Comfort her in any situation of distress,
And of course, the answer was a resounding yes!!!!!

Alas! There was more delay,
Caused by no other than a pandemic,

Much to theirs (and many's) dismay,
Infact... to be exact- it was an epidemic,
Causing postponement to one of the most important days,
But today itself would be worth any delays.

As they say the now is a present,
A gift for always,
Much like the gift of love,
No turning back,
Will fits like a glove,
Honest forever and that's a fact,
Loyalty to the stars above.

So now, finally- today,
Radhi and Tom,
Here is your final scene romcom,
It's finally here,
Against cv19 fear,
Let's whisper to immortalise this to say,
And ever so gratefully;
Happy Wedding Day!

16. The One about the Paternal Past and Present

Who would I be if you were here?
What would have been if you stayed?
What if I never needed to shed a tear?
What if I got the attention I craved?

For years I brushed it off...
Acted strong when I was not,
For years I feigned being tough,
Made out I was fine with my lot,
My life at the time shattered,
Familial home physically tattered,
As a teen all was black or white,
Pretending it all never mattered,
Feigning 'childlikely' carelessness like a kite,
When in reality-I was depleted and low,
Inside everything felt tainted black,
Still don't understand how you could just go?
Walk away and not turn back,
Discard us like a worn out pair of shoes,
Worn for years but ultimately worn out,
No longer needed for original use,
No purpose for walking with and about,
What was your excuse?

To not be there and choosing to walk out?
I'll never know what would have become,
Or the person I would be,
Even what things I would have done,
If your leaving had not mis-shapen me,
The steps I've had to take,
Since you left- I may have walked a different path,
The decisions I had to make,
Would have all been an alternate past,
I know only of one thing that would have been certain,
That on my dear sisters Wedding Day,
My Uncle stepping in as a version,
In the role to give her away,
Was unnecessary- as it would have been you,
In fact, it should have been,
Something for you to do,
As her Father, and the first male kin,
But that's a duty saved for a real Dad,
Not in essence a sperm donor-which was almost all we had,
At least there's nobility in that,
And actually, that may have been better,
Also so there are no memories- nor good nor sad,
Nothing to come flooding back,
When we knew you were gone for good,

No flashes of anger nor attack,
No feelings to be misunderstood,
Misconstrued by memory and absence,
Of the hypothetical,
Only imagining your presence,
Making our own morals and ethical,
May be it would have been easier to come to terms with,
But may be ‘easy’ is just the fantastical myth,
That my heart and mind longs for,
After all, it's the peace within would be the strongest force,
To 'placid-idate' my parents divorce.

17. The One about Living with Pain

Scared of dying,
Or being scared of living,
Or living in pain?
It all feels all the same.

Maybe I should just say scared of it all,
Life skyscrapers me- just feel so small,
Or I guess just scared?

...

Not 'just' actually.
Scared
Scared?
Yep, scared.
There, I've admitted it.
Conceded defeat.

I'll write and repeat it for effect

SCARED.

Scared full stop.

That poetic punctuation feels justified.

Maybe I can justify the word too?

Put it in the middle and isolate it?

SCARED.

Justify the feeling,
That's so reeling,
Real-ing too,
And feeling,
Intertwined,
Reeling like an old school slideshow,
Like a biopic flickers,
On a old school slideshow,
Like the Deen and pearl preview,
That never ends,
Until we meet again,
Or I meet my demise,
And rest my eyes,
For the very last time,
Willing to bet my bottom dime,
It won't be in peace,
But an unrestful sleep,
Maybe, just maybe, instead...

Pieces of regret.

Part two:

I'm also scarred,
Not just scared,
The extra "R'
Euniciates the purrs,
Which ironically only occurs,
After pain,
After rain,
And the storm,
A scar is just a 'physical' form,
From collateral damage,
Serves as a reminder of the trauma,
Mental scars uneasily seen,
In self,
But what was previous,
Would have been seen,
And clear as day of everything that's been.

Part 3:

Fear of flying,

Fear of falling,

And even the icy now,

Needs to dethaw,
What is it though?

What does it boil down to?

Maybe it's just fear of it all?

Feels like a feat to say its fear alone,

Admission of fear is not what the superheroes
of the world are meant to do,
Meant to be strong and save themselves and
also you too.

18.The One about Strength

They colloquially say 'what doesn't kill, makes me stronger',
But I feel weaker,
Still reeling,
And less feeling,
Most impacted is my ability to love,
And patience to devote thereof,
Then comes the guilt,
Destroying confidence built,
I feel like a fail,
Bailing,
And to no avail,
Everything that's gone on,
Battlelines already drawn,
Leaving me bereft,
Nothing is left,
I'm depleted,
Basically emptied,
Hollowed from the war,
Hardest to ignore,
Is my negative self-talk,
I must remind myself nada was built in a Day,
I'm still alive to live and to stay,
Tomorrow is another day and I still remain,
Despite the rain,
Sometimes it is enough to just maintain.

19. The One About The Moment of Vulnerability in Sleep

Each night we lay- still and close,
Mere Inches apart,
As our days slow,
So does our heart,
I feel your presence,
Even your aura maybe,
The proximity and lack of absence,
Looking as idyllic as a sleeping baby,
Laying and lying next to each other,
Becoming one,
Not willing to find another,
And still not done,
I lay inches apart from you-
Both safe and sound-

If only it were always this way,
A way to still the threat and strafe,
That laying inches apart poses,
Knowing that life was never meant to be all roses.

19. The One about Musically Intrusive Thoughts

I feel like a broken record.
I play on repeat with no ability to skip.
Repeated single cassette- even though it hurts,
With every beat a little more,
I'm certain people are bugged by it,
I think the only way to stop it,
Would be to do something drastic,
Something extreme still feels like would result- in a deafening silence,
If only for a moment or a beat,
Of redemption,
Feel frozen in fear,
Can only hum along to the painful tune of anxiety,
There is no better album or way to change track,
At these times I have to remind myself to be kind,
What lyrics would I sing to outsing someone elses- or anybody else's- anxiety track...

Even just provide another beat or lyric,
Knowing full well just how it feels,

If it was so easy- I would just change the whole album,
Switch to another turntable,
But if it was as simple as that?
I would do it in a heartbeat,
But its not and that's why I can't,
So I shouldn't berate myself.
For it seldom helps but I can't help but hum along to it...

I wish I felt I had a choice.

20. The One about Fighting the Good Fight

I'm a lover, never a fighter,
Only fighting for what I love...

I've cried too many tears over you,
It's time to stop,
It's been the time to stop,
Stop.
Breathe and let go,
Nothings simple as that though,
Of course- nothing ever is,
Nothing worth fighting is,
But when will the fighting stop?
If ever?

At what point is enough is enough?
We've burned each other before,
Said sorry once or twice more,
Never seem to learn,
Or yield new answers,
Knowing the worst of me,
I've let you see,
Yet vulnerability is no excuse,
It all meshes into a mess,
Don't know if it's worth the stress,

Or worse...
If it ever was?!

21.The One for Anyone With Everyday Struggles

Less is more,
Some days we struggle to brush our teeth,
Or brush our hair,
Put a face on,
Much less our mask.

Some is enough,
Its too much to do all,
We cannot be perfect,
Idealism is a sycophants cure,
A job worth doing is worth doing right.

Bollocks to that,
Don't succumb to that life trap!
We are not robots,
Have some humanity,
And compassion for yourself,
Don't beat yourself up if you can't,
You are doing the best you can- let's all chant!

Hush, your inner critic,
If it was easy it would be done,
But it's not, so why rush to berate?
You're trying, and that's enough!

Why do we treat others so well,

Yet seldom the same level of love for
ourselves?
Be your own best friend,
It's worth it,
Can't pour from empty cup,
Otherwise you'd be a mug!
Practice what you preach,
Truly love what you teach.

Self-love may just be the most important love of all.

www.ingramcontent.com/pod-product-compliance
Lightning Source LLC
Chambersburg PA
CBHW051740130826
49812CB00033B/935
* 9 7 8 9 3 5 7 4 4 4 9 8 9 *